About the playwright

Greg Gould is an Australian playwright.

His short plays have been performed throughout Australia, as well as in New Zealand, the United States, Ireland, Canada, India, the United Arab Emirates, and the Philippines.

He has won multiple Best Production, People's Choice, and Best Script awards at Short+Sweet Play Festivals around the world. In 2019, his play *Last Drinks* was a First Place Winner in the Smith & Kraus and True Acting Institute 10 Minute Play Contest for Theatres and Playwrights.

Greg's first full length-play, *The Inheritance*, was produced by Budding Theatre in 2017. His script for the play was nominated for Best Original Work at the 2017 Canberra Area Theatre Awards. In 2019 he was nominated for the same award for his short play *The Hold-Up*.

In 2019 his short play *Fallout* won first prize in the New York City Audio Theatre Writing Contest.

To see more of Greg's work, go to www.nowordfor.com.

LAST DRINKS

and other short plays

LAST DRINKS

and other short plays

GREG GOULD

Blemish Books ■ Canberra

First published 2020 by
Blemish Books
Canberra, Australia
www.blemishbooks.com.au

Copyright © Greg Gould

The Australian Copyright Act 1968 (Act) allows a maximum of one chapter or 10% of this book, whichever is the greater, to be copied by any educational institution for its educational purposes provided that that educational institution (or the body that administers it) has given a remuneration notice to Copyright Agency Limited (CAL) under the Act. For details of the CAL license for educational institutions, contact CAL at info@copyright.com.au

Without prior permission of the publisher, no part of this publication may be reproduced, stored in a retrieval system, or transmitted in any form or by any means (electronic, mechanical, photocopying, recording, or otherwise).

Performance royalties
The playwright grants permission for these plays to be performed royalty-free. You do not need to purchase a license to use these plays in your productions. This includes amateur and professional productions as well as auditions, staged readings, and informal readings. While you do not have to pay a fee to use these plays, the playwright loves being notified of any public performances. If you produce one or more of these plays, let us know at greg@nowordfor.com.

Diversity pledge
The playwright encourages anyone producing and casting these works to consider performers from diverse backgrounds, including for roles where a character's ethnic or cultural background, age, gender, sexuality, or disability need not be specified. Character genders and ages are suggestions only. Feel free to mix it up!

Previous publications
'Last Drinks' first appeared in *Best Ten-Minute Plays of 2019* (True Acting Institute), March 2019.
'Stargazers' first appeared in *Stage It! 3: Twenty 10-Minute Plays* (ed. Frank Blocker), April 2019.

Cover design by Sengsavane Chounramany (www.sengsavane.wordpress.com).

ISBN: 978-0-6482198-1-1

A catalogue record for this book is available from the National Library of Australia

For Les and Artie, my co-writers in life.

Thank you to the many actors, directors and producers that have brought these plays to life around the world.

Special thanks to my frequent collaborators and supporters: Alex Broun, Maggie Allen, Kirsty Budding and Budding Entertainment, Peter Fock, Rahael Hogan, Michael Ubrihien, Philip Meddows, Helen Way, Arne Sjosetd, Rob de Fries, Brendan Kelly, Jess Waterhouse, Short+Sweet, and the Canberra Ten-Min Write Club — this collection would not exist without you.

— Greg Gould

Contents

Last Drinks	1
Stargazers	15
The Hold-Up	29
Smart Jimmy, Slow Bob	43
Fallout	55
The Truth About Mum and Dad	68
The Unexpected	82
Sexy Beth's Giant Dildo Collection	96

LAST DRINKS

Cast

Mel, 30s female; she's having a bad day

Ben, 30s male; every day is a bad day

Setting

A bar

Time

Saturday afternoon

Synopsis

A woman whose partners keep dying meets a man who can't seem to die. Did destiny bring these two tragic souls together?

A shabby pub. Ben sits at the bar nursing a beer. He's contemplating life (as people do in bars). Suddenly he pulls out a bottle of pills, takes one out, washes it down with a swig of beer. Then he sits, waiting.

Mel enters. She's agitated, distraught, and wearing a wedding dress. She sits at the other end of the bar.

Mel: Vodka. Straight up.

The drink arrives and she downs it.

Mel: Keep 'em coming.

Mel notices Ben looking at her, intrigued. Mel looks away.

Mel: Don't.

Ben: I got to ask.

Mel: No. It's not my wedding day.

Ben: (*confused*) Right.

Beat.

Ben: So …?

Mel: Really?

Ben: What?

Mel: You're really gonna do this?

Ben: Bride in a bar. Got to ask.

Mel: If you must know, I've been at a funeral.

Ben: Funeral?

Mel: Yep.

She downs another drink.

Beat.

Ben: That only raises more questions.

Mel: You asked.

Ben: Why would you wear a wedding dress to a funeral?

Mel: Last request.

Ben: Hell of a last request.

Mel: Wasn't exactly made under the best of circumstances.

Ben: Who would want that?

Mel: James would. My husband. Or at least he was going to be my husband. He didn't quite make it.

Ben: (*understanding*) Right.

Mel: Yep. Dropped dead right at the altar. Ceremony hadn't even started. By the time I got to him, he was all but gone. But he held on. Said he wanted to see me in my wedding dress. Said I was the most beautiful bride in the world. Then he said the other thing: 'Keep the dress on, babe. Wear it at the funeral'.

Ben: Jesus.

Mel: I know. The doc reckons it was the endorphins talking. Probably didn't even know what he was saying.

Ben: But you did it anyway?

Mel: Of course. It was his last request. And everyone heard it. The priest. The best man. The bridesmaids. Even his mother heard it. Old bat's deaf as a doornail, but she hears that fucking request from three rows back.

Ben: So how …?

Mel: Heart attack. At 34. Who the fuck has a heart attack at 34?

Ben: (*envious*) Son of a bitch.

Mel: You know the messed-up thing? I wasn't going to do it.

Ben: Do what?

Mel: The wedding. I was halfway across the parking lot when they found me. Gone. But then this. God, I'm such a bitch.

Ben: You weren't to know.

Mel: Still. It's so low. I was just going to leave him standing there. Like a schmuck. He was so excited. Been asking me to marry him for years. But I kept knocking him back. Finally, I say yes, and this happens. Maybe he knew. Maybe that's why.

Ben: Nah, shitty timing is all. Chances are he died happily oblivious.

Mel: That's even worse.

Ben: You're being too hard on yourself. You didn't want to get married, so you acted. End of the day you were trying to do the right thing.

Mel: Till he died.

Ben: Bad luck. Nothing more.

Mel: I just can't believe this happened again.

Ben: You've been married before?

Mel: No. I mean the death thing. This is the fourth guy I've been with that's keeled over.

Ben: You're shitting me?

Mel: The first was Ivan Taylor. High school boyfriend. He lived two towns over. One night he borrowed his dad's car to come see me and *BAM*, T-boned by a semi. Dead. Second guy was Glen Walsh. Nice guy. Met at uni. Went on a romantic weekend to Thredbo and *BAM*, he skis straight into a snow machine. Dead.

Ben: Accidents. Could happen to anyone.

Mel: Then there was Jason Mills. Met at work. He fell out of a hot-air balloon.

Ben: Bullshit.

Mel: True story. He took me up for my twenty-fifth. Two thousand feet in the air, he leans out to take a selfie … and … gone. Landed on power lines. Burnt to a crisp.

Ben: That's pretty unlikely.

Mel: I swear, I'm cursed. You know what they call me? 'The Widow Maker.' So stupid. Doesn't even make sense.

Ben: Surprised the cops didn't get suss on you. Three boyfriends. Three deaths.

Mel: Oh, they did. That how I met James. He was a detective.

Ben: Fuck off!

Mel: I tried to tell him. I warned him. But he wouldn't listen. Said I was being superstitious. He even sent me to a shrink. She said I was a paranoid delusional. Guess I proved them both wrong.

Ben: How is this even possible?

Mel: Dunno. Must've fucked over the wrong person in a past life or something.

Ben: I'm so sorry.

Mel: Not your fault. I should never have said yes. Big mistake. But everyone kept saying 'It'll be fine, Mel. It'll be fine'. What do they know? I'm destined to be alone. Destined to die alone. Destined to … get shit-faced. (*downs a drink*)

Ben: No. I mean I'm sorry you have to be here for this.

Mel: For what?

Ben: For this. My death. I've come here to die. To have my last drink.

Mel: You've lost me. Jesus, how many of these have I had?

Ben: I took a pill. I should be dead any minute. Actually, I should be dead now. Supposed to be quick.

Mel: You're serious?

Ben: Yep.

Mel: Jesus! Should I call someone? An ambulance?

Ben: No, don't. I've thought about this. A lot. I've tried many times.

Mel: How many?

Ben: Twelve.

Mel: Twelve?! Fuck, you mustn't be very good! (*cringes*) Sorry. That came out bad. I'm just saying after so many tries, maybe this isn't what you want.

Ben: No. I'm certain of it. Things just keep getting in the way.

Mel: What kind of things?

Ben: All sorts. Odd things. Last week I drove my car off a cliff. Hundred-foot drop straight into the ocean. Walked away with nothing but a bruised collarbone.

Mel: How?

Ben: Police Rescue was training on the beach below.

Mel: Get out.

Ben: Last year I tried the whole connect-the-hose-to-the-exhaust-pipe thing. Everything was going great. Car was full of fumes. Head was spinning. Then a truck crashes through the garage door. Driver had a stroke. I wake up in the hospital, fine.

Mel: No way!

Ben: I know. It's crazy. Nothing works. I'm like the Frank Spencer of suicide attempts. Stupid shit just keeps happening.

Mel: Gun?

Ben: Faulty ammunition.

Mel: Electrocution?

Ben: Took the toaster into the bath. Whole block went dark. I didn't feel a tingle.

Mel: Slit wrists?

Ben: Went out bush. Was miraculously found by the SES who happened to be searching for a lost bushwalker. They still haven't found him.

Mel: Drug overdose?

Ben: Jehovah's Witness

Mel: (*confused*) What?

Ben: They came knocking at the door.

Mel: Base jump?

Ben: Leapt from a sixth-floor window, landed in a trailer full of mattresses.

Mel: Fuck off! That doesn't happen.

Ben: It happened.

Mel: What about stepping in front of a bus?

Ben: Broken arm the first time, broken leg the second. Otherwise fine.

Mel: Hanging? No, let me guess. Rope snapped.

Ben: Actually no. But the beam I tied it to did. Brought down the entire first floor of my sister's apartment. I was unscathed.

Mel: Get fucked!

Ben: I know. It's absurd. I even paid a professional hitman to take me out. Dickhead went to the wrong house. Killed my neighbour instead.

Mel: Jesus. You're like Bruce Willis in that movie. The one where he's all invincible.

Ben: *Unbreakable.*

Mel: Nah. The other one. With the ghosts.

Ben: I'm pretty sure you mean *Unbreakable*.

Mel: Whatever. You're totally that guy. Un-killable. It's insane.

Ben: Glad you find it entertaining.

Mel: Not just entertaining. I am in awe. The sheer persistence of it. It's admirable.

Ben: You know the weird thing? This is what I live for now. It's the only reason I get out of bed in the morning. I need to know. You know? I need to find out how it ends. (*picks up the pill bottle*) What the fuck is wrong with these things? Should kill a horse.

Mel: Aren't we the pair? 'The Widow Maker' and 'The Invincible Man'. Destiny, I salute you! You've got one fucked up sense of humour.

Beat.

Ben: You believe in that stuff? Destiny? Fate?

Mel: Only explanation. I don't give a shit what anyone says. Coincidence can only explain so much.

Ben: So, you think we're supposed to be here? To meet? Like this?

Mel: Makes sense. Who knows? Perhaps all the men in my life died just so I would meet you.

Ben: And maybe that's why I can't die.

Mel: There is a kind of poetry to it. A sick, depraved kind of poetry. But poetry nonetheless.

Ben: Would explain the impotent pills.

Mel: And why I'm wearing this stupid dress. You wouldn't have talked to me otherwise.

Ben: You do look beautiful.

Mel: Thanks. You're not too bad yourself. For a manic depressive.

Ben: Says the paranoid delusional.

They laugh. There's a beat filled with attraction.

Ben: So, what now?

Mel: You like hot-air balloons?

Ben: Never been in one.

Mel: Maybe you should. Maybe instead of trying to kill yourself all the time, you should live a little.

Ben: And maybe you should stop feeling guilty about things you can't control. Let go a little.

Mel: Maybe I should.

Beat. More attraction. They move closer.

Mel: We should kiss.

Ben: You think?

Mel: I dunno. Might be the vodka talking. But it feels right. (*they lean in close*) Though I should warn you. This doesn't usually end well.

Ben: Don't worry. I'm invincible. Remember?

They share a lingering kiss.

Mel: Wow. That was actually pretty good.

Ben: Thanks.

Beat as they smile stupidly at one another. They lean in to kiss again.

Ben drops dead.

Mel: Oh, c'mon. Really? Really?!

Beat.

Mel picks up a drink, downs it.

Mel: Another!

ENDS

STARGAZERS

Cast

Danny, teen male; a weird teenager / alien

Becky, teen female; a bored teenager

Dr Ludwig, 50s male; a nutty professor / alien

Setting

An isolated field

Time

Night

Synopsis

When a romantic evening under the stars is rudely interrupted by his eccentric father, a small-town teenager is forced to make a decision that is out of this world.

Enter Danny and Becky. Danny is leading Becky by the hand. Becky is wearing a blindfold.

Becky: Are we there yet?

Danny: Almost.

Becky: Can I at least see where we're going?

Danny: That would ruin the surprise.

Becky: This is so stupid. If I fall and ruin these jeans, I'll be pissed.

Danny: You'll be fine. In fact, here we are.

Becky takes the blindfold off, looks around.

Becky: We're in a field.

Danny: Surprise.

Becky: Why are we in a field? You're not gonna make me tip a cow or something?

Danny: Look up.

Becky: This is kinda weird.

Danny: Just look.

Becky looks up to see an enchanting, glittering star-filled sky.

Becky: Holy shit.

Danny: Cool, huh?

Becky: It's … it's …

Danny: Beautiful?

Becky: Big. I was gonna say big.

Danny: New moon tonight.

Becky: What happened to the old one?

Danny: It's rising and setting with the sun. That's why the sky's so bright. Look. You can see the Double Cluster. And the Lagoon Nebula.

Becky: How do you know this stuff?

Danny: My dad.

Becky: Of course. The nutty professor.

Danny: Black holes. Planets. Nebulae. He lives for this stuff.

Becky: Is that why he's so kooky?

Danny: You think he's kooky?

Becky: Strangest damn science teacher I've ever had.

Danny: He just wants to understand. What's out there. How it works.

Becky: Oh god. You didn't bring me here for that?

Danny: For what?

Becky: The space talk. Why are we here? Are we alone? Will I be abducted by aliens and probed in the you-know-what?

Danny: You're not curious?

Becky: About probing?

Danny: About the stars.

Becky: Not really. I mean, I look up and it's amazing. But it's big. And far away. So far it doesn't matter.

Danny: Doesn't matter? It's everything.

Becky: Not everything.

Danny: Everything that's not here.

Becky: Which for all we know could be a whole lot of nothing.

Danny: Believe me, it's not nothing.

Becky: Yeah? How do you know?

Danny: Statistics and probability. Space is infinite. No start. No end. Its size is incomprehensible. Yet if even the smallest fraction of it contains 'something' …

Becky: So, you believe in little green men?

Danny: Not green men per se.

Becky: Alright. So why haven't we seen this 'something'?

Danny: Statistics and probability. Space is huge. The chances of two sentient organisms existing at the same time, within reasonable proximity. The odds are astronomical. Literally.

Becky: You sound like him. The nutty professor.

Danny: We are related.

Becky: Is this really why you brought me here? To gaze at stars?

Danny: You don't like them?

Becky: Honestly? I'm more interested with what's happening down here. I've seen you. Watching me. In class. On the bus.

Danny: Really?

Becky: I don't know about black holes or nebulae. But I know when a boy likes me.

Danny: Fascinating.

Becky: 'Fascinating'? God, you are so weird.

Danny: I'm not that weird.

Becky: You're super weird. First day of school. You shook hands with every single person you met. That was weird. Mrs Pattinson. You asked her if she and her guide dog had a 'symbiotic relationship'. That was weird. Charlotte. You gave her a goat for her birthday. A live one. That was weird. But you're lucky. I like weird. Though it still doesn't explain why you brought out me here.

Danny: I just needed to know.

Becky: Know what?

Danny: If I found what I was looking for.

Becky: And what's that?

Danny: A connection. To see if we're compatible.

Becky: Compatible? You mean … (*she kisses him*) … compatible? (*beat*) Seem pretty compatible to me.

Danny: Indeed.

The lights of an approaching car fall across them.

Becky: What the hell?

Danny: Oh god …

Becky: Is that …? What's he doing here?

Danny: I have no idea.

Enter Dr Ludwig, exuberant.

Ludwig: Danny! Thank Jupiter. You weren't at the house.

Danny: Yeah, I was just—

Ludwig: Did you receive the communication?

Danny: What communication?

Ludwig: Just came in. Our window has narrowed. The timetable has been advanced.

Danny: Advanced? To when?

Ludwig: Now, boy. Now! Have you got your locator?

Danny: Yeah, but—

Ludwig: Excellent. Initiate power. Signals at full strength.

Becky: What at full strength?

Ludwig: Who's the female?

Danny: This is Becky.

Ludwig: Who?

Becky: Becky, Dr Ludwig. I have you for physics …

Ludwig: She can't be here.

Danny: We were just talking.

Ludwig: No time for talk! Sorry dear. I'm sure your parents want you home …

Becky: Actually, Mum said I could stay out till eleven.

Dr Ludwig starts frantically pacing the stage, waving around his locator device.

Becky: What is he doing?

Danny: Calibrating.

Becky: For what?

Danny: To leave.

Becky: Wait. You're moving? When?

Danny: Now. Apparently.

Becky: Now! But you can't leave! I just … we just … You're the only cool thing in this town!

Danny: Sorry. I thought I had more time.

Ludwig: Aha! We've got a lock! Suit up, boy. (*beat*) She's still here.

Danny: She was just leaving.

Becky: No, I wasn't. I don't care how weird you are. You can't kiss me then just take off.

Ludwig: You kissed her? Where?

Danny: On the mouth.

Ludwig: Fascinating. What was it like?

Becky: Excuse me?

Danny: Nice.

Becky: (*touched*) You thought it was nice?

Ludwig: Any physiological changes?

Danny: Increased heart rate. Clammy hands.

Ludwig: Skin irritation? Numbness?

Danny: Not yet …

Becky: What kind of kisser do you think I am?

Ludwig: Damn. We're out of swabs. We'll take a sample later. Full diagnostics. We'll need to eliminate any contagions.

Becky: Contagions? Danny. What the hell is going on?

Danny: Nothing. It's fine …

Ludwig: That's right, dear. Everything is fine. In fact, if you could look this way …

Dr Ludwig shines a neural inhibiter in Becky's eyes (think Men in Black*). She's paralysed.*

Danny: Dad! No! You can't keep zapping people like that!

Ludwig: She'll be fine. Besides, after tonight, we're done zapping. Thank Jupiter. These vessels. So restrictive. And itchy. The skin. The hair. The constant leaking of liquids and gas.

Danny: They're not that bad.

Ludwig: They're intolerable. Never felt so dense.

Danny: Their bodies are lacking. But they're smart.

Ludwig: Smart! Last week a man lit a cigarette at a fuel station. Blew up half a city block.

Danny: They've built cities. Culture. Art.

Ludwig: They've also built bombs. Which they drop on their cities, culture, and art.

Danny: They're not all like that.

Ludwig: No. Just enough. (*off locator*) You getting these?

Danny: They're coming in fast.

Ludwig:	Huddle close. We can save energy on the transfer.
Danny:	I don't think I can.
Ludwig:	Humour? At a time like this! They have rubbed off on you.
Danny:	No. I mean. I think I want to stay.
Ludwig:	Here? Are you mad!? You've seen what these creatures do.
Danny:	I have. And you're right. They're violent. Lazy. Illogical. But they care about one another. Love one another. Despite how weird they can be.
Ludwig:	Great Jupiter. You've gone native.
Danny:	That was our job.
Ludwig:	No, boy! Observe and report. Observe. And report. What's the commander gonna say? You're risking your entire future even considering this.
Danny:	What future? There's nothing out there.
Ludwig:	You know that's not true.
Danny:	Might as well be. How long have we been searching? What have we found? A slug. Some moss. A blob of mucus on a dead rock.

Ludwig: Yes. But imagine what we'll find next. It could be incredible. It could be divine. It could be … like us …

Danny: I don't want divine. I want real.

Beat.

Ludwig: You know they consume living organisms.

Danny: I know.

Ludwig: They excrete waste through their reproductive organs.

Danny: I know.

Ludwig: They don't know how gravity works.

Danny: They'll figure it out. Eventually.

Beat.

Ludwig: Very well.

Danny: Really?

Ludwig: It's a free galaxy. For now. Who am I to tell you how to live? Or in what body.

Danny: What about the commander?

Ludwig: I'll say they ate you. Apparently, that's still a thing.

Danny: Thanks, Dad.

Danny holds Dr Ludwig tight. Dr Ludwig is embarrassed by the gesture.

Ludwig: You know I'm not your father, right? You're a thousand years older than me.

Danny: I know.

Ludwig: You're a weird guy, Danny.

Danny: I know.

Blinking lights of an approaching UFO.

Ludwig: Well, that's me. Best of luck! Remember, the green light means go. Ice cream is not a fertiliser. And never discuss religion at the dinner table. You'll starve before you convince them! Farewell.

Dr Ludwig exits.

Beat.

Danny places a hand on Becky's shoulder.

Danny: You can look now.

Becky: We're in a field. Why are we in a field?

Danny: Look up.

Becky looks up to see a sky full of glittering stars.

Becky: Holy shit.

Danny: Cool huh?

Becky: Yeah. It's … it's …

Danny: Big?

Becky: Beautiful. I was gonna say beautiful.

He takes her hand. They look up at the sky.

ENDS

THE HOLD-UP

Cast

Customer, 20s male; philosophy student, bit of a slacker

Clerk, 40s male; street-smart, clever

Robber, 30s male; thuggish but also insightful

Setting

An inner-city convenience store

Time

A weekday, lunchtime

Synopsis

When a slacker philosophy student ducks into an inner-city convenience store to spy on his girlfriend, he suddenly finds himself in the middle of a not-so-philosophical hold-up.

The clerk staffs the counter of an inner-city convenience store. We hear a door chime as the customer enters. He wears a hoodie and sunglasses. He hovers by a flower display, eyes fixed on something offstage.

Clerk: Hey, mister. (*beat*) Mister.

Customer: Me?

Clerk: Yeah. What are you doing over there?

Customer: Nothing. Just standing.

Clerk: Yeah? You look dodgy. You look like you're going to rob me.

Customer: What? I'm not gonna rob you. I'm just … hiding.

Clerk: From what? Cops?

Customer: Cops? No, my … girlfriend …

Clerk: Robber, stalker, whatever. You're creeping out the customers.

Customer: What customers?

Clerk: Okay. You're creeping me out. You gotta go.

Customer: C'mon, man. I'm just— I was going to surprise her. For lunch. But I turn up and she's having coffee. With some guy. Who is that guy?

Clerk: Store is for paying customers. Buy something or leave.

Customer: Seriously? (*beat*) Fine. Just give me this.

He grabs a packet of gum from the counter display.

Clerk: Two fifty.

Customer: For gum?

Clerk: Not just gum. Raspberry Crush.

The customer reluctantly pulls out a fifty-dollar note and slaps it on the table.

Clerk: Yeah. That won't work.

Customer: What? Why?

Clerk: Too big.

Customer: Too big?

Clerk: Too big. Can't change it. Buy more.

Customer: More? I don't even want this!

Clerk: Then have a nice day.

Customer: Fine. (*grabs a handful of gum packets*) Just give me these.

Clerk: Twenty dollars.

Customer: Twenty! (*hands over money*) Can I stand here now?

Clerk: Please.

The customer jams some gum in his mouth, takes up sentry position looking out the window. Beat. The clerk strolls over to join him.

Clerk: So, which …?

Customer: Redhead. By the door.

Clerk: Oh, nice. Professional.

Customer: I guess.

Clerk: Yeah. That's a shame.

Customer: Aye?

Clerk: Woman like that. You won't have her for long.

Customer: What do you know about it?

Clerk: Seven years I've worked this dump. I see all kinds: lawyers, bankers, hookers, bums. Last week I caught a guy trying to take a dump in the freezer aisle. I know people.

Customer: You thought I was a robber.

Clerk: Actually, I thought you were a pervert. Robber seemed more polite.

Customer: What about this guy? Lawyer, right?

Clerk: Oh, yeah. Expensive suit. Slick hair. Strong eye contact. All the hallmarks of a professional liar.

Customer: I knew it. Bet it's that Craig guy. She's always talking about him. Owns a Porsche.

Clerk: So?

Customer: That's what she said. 'Craig owns a Porsche'. She tried to sound cool about it, but I could tell she was impressed.

Clerk: She doesn't care about his car.

Customer: That a fact?

Clerk: Look at her. She's smart. Independent. Capable. And she's repulsed by him.

Customer: She is?

Clerk: Look at her. See how she sits? Arms crossed, legs bent to the street. See how she turns her shoulders. Keeps her hands close to her body. She can't wait to get away from him.

Customer: You can't know that.

Clerk: Believe me, I know.

Beat. The customer is confused.

Customer: But you said I was going to lose her.

Clerk: You will. But not to him. You'll lose her cos you're a slacker. You've got nothing to offer.

Customer: I got plenty.

Clerk: Please. How old are you? 30?

Customer: 28.

Clerk: 28 and wearing sweats in the middle of the day.

Customer: These are corduroy.

Clerk: Let me guess: Student? Postgrad? Arts?

Customer: Philosophy.

Clerk: Philosophy: the study of why smart people do stupid things.

Customer: No. That's psychology. Philosophy's why wise people do foolish things.

Clerk: So that's where you met this girl? At uni? Only now she's moved on. Got a job. Purpose. Meanwhile, you're holding on to what was. Delaying the inevitable.

Customer: I'm not delaying anything. I'm doing a PhD.

Clerk: In philosophy.

Customer: Still.

Clerk: Please, I know a slacker when I see one. Goalless. Apathetic. Easily manipulated.

Customer: I am not easily manipulated.

Clerk: Says the man with twenty dollars' worth of Raspberry Crush in his pocket …

Customer: You don't know what you're talking about.

Clerk: I know you should be over there with your girlfriend. Not hiding in here like a perv.

Customer: She can handle herself. Besides, I hate those guys. With their suits and cars and slick … everything. I always feel so …

Clerk: Intimidated? Inept? Pathetic?

Customer: Stupid.

Clerk: Sport, there are only two kinds of stupid in the world: those who look for trouble and those who don't prepare for it.

Customer: Kant?

Clerk: Machiavelli.

Customer: (*impressed*) Huh.

The door chime sounds again as the robber enters the store. He too is dressed in sunglasses and a hoodie. He hangs suspiciously by the counter.

Clerk: So, what are you going to do?

Customer: What do you care?

Clerk: I don't. But I need to know how you're going to react.

Customer: To what?

Clerk: To this. We're about to get robbed.

Customer: Dude, not every guy who wears a hoodie is a crook.

Clerk: No. But this one is. Just keep your mouth shut. He's a pro. (*to the robber*) Can I help you, sir?

The robber pulls out a knife.

Robber: Yeah. You can empty the register.

Customer: Holy shit!

Robber: And the safe.

Clerk: No problem. Whole tray?

Robber: Just the cash.

Clerk: Bundled?

Robber: Just bag it.

Clerk: Change?

Robber: Keep the shrapnel. (*points high offstage*) That thing on?

Clerk: Keep your head down, you'll be fine.

Robber: Not your first stick-up?

Clerk: I've been doing this a while.

Robber: Well, I appreciate the professionalism. Nice change from the usual hysterics.

Clerk: I'm just glad you're not some jacked-up junky with a gun.

Robber: Mate, you don't have to tell me. Number of dickheads I see running around like it's 'Grand Theft fucking Auto'. Make the rest of us look like a bunch of morons. (*to customer*) What's your story, chief? You gotta take a piss?

Customer: No. I went before I left the house …

Robber: Yeah? You gonna get in on this?

Customer: (*confused*) What?

Robber: You gonna empty your pockets, or what?

Customer: Right.

The customer quickly empties his pockets on to counter.

Robber: Sweet Jesus. Gum much? What have you got? Halitosis?

Customer: What?

Clerk: Halitosis. Bad breath. (*to robber*) Philosophy student.

Robber: (*understanding*) Oh.

Customer: I just like gum.

Clerk: He doesn't. He's easily manipulated.

Robber: Looks the type.

Customer: What type?

Robber: Weak. Demure. Afraid of your own shadow.

Clerk: Bingo.

Customer: I am not demure.

Robber: Mate. I see it all the time. Guys like you. Jam a knife in your face and you hand over cash faster than a virgin at a strip club.

Customer: Of course, I would. You've got a bloody knife!

Clerk: Guy across the street doesn't.

Robber: What guy?

Customer: There's no guy.

Clerk: The one having coffee with his girlfriend.

Robber: Yeah? (*goes to window*) Which one? Fatty by the window?

Clerk: Redhead. By the door.

Customer: (*to clerk*) Dude.

Robber: Hot damn. Ripe. She's with you?

Clerk: I know, right?

Customer: (*to clerk*) Dude.

Robber: Who's the stiff in the suit?

Clerk: That's Craig. He owns a Porsche.

Robber: Of course, he does. Twat. Sure wants to bone your missus though.

Clerk: Big time.

Customer: Is this really appropriate banter for a robbery?

Robber: She don't look keen though.

Clerk: Nope.

Robber: That begs the question: What you doing here? Why aren't you over there telling 'Captain Cockhead' to back off your woman.

Customer: First, she doesn't need me to do anything. Second—

Clerk: He's a slacker. And a perv.

Customer: I'm not a perv.

Robber: You know what I'd do? I'd walk over there smack that smug fucker in the back of the head with a crowbar?

Customer: Really? A crowbar?

Robber: Or a chair.

Customer: No offence, but I don't take advice from criminals.

Robber: Hey, I might be a crook, but I was in love once. Woman was electric. Stabbed me seven times in my sleep. God, I miss her.

Beat.

Customer: Can we just maybe wrap this up?

Robber: Why? You got somewhere to be?

Customer: No. I just think there's a finite amount of time you should spend robbing a place.

The robber moves in on the customer, shows him the knife.

Robber: What are you saying, chief? You think I don't know how to do a stick-up? You think I'm some pimple-nosed pin-dick fresh out of juvie?

Customer: What? No, I just …

Beat. The robber bursts out laughing.

Robber: Look at this guy. Shit his pants. You know what? When I'm done here, I'm gonna go over there, smack that smug fucker myself. Think your missus would like that? Think she'd like to see how a real man handles himself.

Customer: You stay away from her.

Robber: Or what, smart guy? What's a piss-ant like you gonna do about it?

Customer: I'll …

Robber: What?

Customer: I'll …

Robber: Yeah?

Customer: I'll …

The clerk pulls a crowbar out from behind the counter and clocks the robber on the head. The robber collapses to the ground, unconscious.

Customer: Holy shit!

Clerk: Told ya. Two kinds of stupid. (*beat*) You should get out of here.

Customer: Won't the cops want to talk to me?

Clerk: Probably. But you got somewhere to be. Don't you?

Customer: Yeah. Yeah, I do.

The customer grabs the crowbar, starts marching out. Then he has second thoughts. He stops, turns back, hands the crowbar back to the clerk. He grabs a bunch of flowers instead.

Clerk: Not so stupid after all.

Customer: Not today.

The customer makes to leave but stops when the clerk clears his throat. Beat.

Clerk: (*off flowers*) That'll be thirty dollars.

Customer: Seriously?!

ENDS

SMART JIMMY, SLOW BOB

Cast

Smart Jimmy, 30s male; sharp-witted gangster

Slow Bob, 20s male; Jimmy's dim-witted brother

Sally, 30s female; Nick's sister

Setting

Intensive care room

Time

Night

Synopsis

After his idiot brother messes up a hit for the boss, a slick gangster must step in to clean up the mess. But when the would-be victim's sister turns up, his loyalties to 'family' are put to the test.

A plain hospital room filled with the beep-beep-beep of a heart monitoring unit. A young man lies motionless on the bed, heavily bandaged. Bob sits in a chair beside him, his face in his hands. Enter Smart Jimmy. He goes straight to Bob.

Jimmy: Bobby?

Bob: Jimmy!

They hug, then Jimmy worriedly gives Bob a once over, checking for cuts, bruises – any signs of damage.

Jimmy: I just heard. You alright?

Bob: Yeah, I'm fine.

Jimmy: You sure? You look pale.

Bob: Nah, I'm good. Really.

Jimmy: Thank God. (*beat*) So?

Bob: Things didn't go right, Jimmy.

Jimmy: No shit. What happened?

Bob: Well, I went to the kid's place, like you said, and I parked out front. And I sat there for like an hour, you know, just hanging around, drinking a Coke, listening to the radio—

Jimmy: Get to the point, Bobby.

Bob: So eventually the kid comes out and starts walking down the street. So, I start the car and I follow him around the corner … I pull up beside him … take out my gun and …

Jimmy: And?

Bob: And this taxi …

Jimmy: Taxi?

Bob: Yeah. This taxi. Just comes out of nowhere and *BAM*! Hits him. Like really hits him. Didn't even see it coming.

Jimmy: You're shitting me?

Bob: I swear to God.

Jimmy: So, you didn't do this?

Bob: No.

Jimmy: Jesus. (*laughs*) Is this kid having a bad day or what? So, what'd you do?

Bob: I called the ambulance.

Jimmy: You what?

Bob: I called the ambulance.

Jimmy: You called the—? Why would you do that?

Bob: I dunno … there were all these people yelling 'Call an ambulance, call an ambulance' … and the taxi was all smashed up … and the kid just lying there and …

Jimmy: Jesus, Bobby, you had one job. Just one: kill the kid. You weren't supposed to become his fairy-fucking-godmother. God damn it. Next thing you'll tell me you rode in the ambulance with him?

Bob's face drops.

Jimmy: You didn't?

Bob can't hide his shame.

Jimmy: Jesus!

Bob: I panicked!

Jimmy: Of course, you panicked. You have the brain capacity of a hamster. God damn it, Bobby, this shit can't keep happening. What's the boss gonna say?

Bob: He's gonna be pretty pissed.

Jimmy: Damn right he is. But he's not gonna be pissed at you, is he? No. He's gonna be pissed at me. Because I'm the fool who told him that my idiot brother could follow simple instructions.

Bob: I'm sorry, Jimmy. I really am.

Jimmy: Look, let's just clean this up and get out of here. Okay? Can we do that?

Bob: Yeah.

Jimmy moves to cover the door. Bob takes out his gun and points it at the victim's head.

Jimmy: Whoa. What the hell!?

Bob: What?

Jimmy: Look around, moron. You can't just pull out a gun and shoot someone in the middle of a hospital. Think, Bobby. Think. Jesus. Use a pillow or something.

Bob puts the gun away, opens a closet. It's full of pillows in various colours.

Bob: What colour?

Jimmy: What colour? Seriously? Are you trying to shit me? It doesn't matter what colour. Just grab a damned a pillow and hold it over the kid's face till he stops breathing. Okay? (*muttering to himself*) What colour?

Bob grabs a pillow, holds it over the victim's face. He suddenly pulls it back.

Bob: I can't do it.

Jimmy: What do you mean you can't do it? Of course, you can do it. He's an invalid. A toddler could do it.

Bob: But look at him. He's all busted up and broken. I've seen some crazy things, Jimmy, but I ain't ever seen anyone survive a crash like that. I think he's supposed to live, you know, like someone's looking out for him. (*beat*) Besides, he looks like Squirt.

Jimmy: What?

Bob: Squirt. You know, the little dog we had when we were kids. He was fluffy brown and really liked cheese.

Jimmy: What the hell are you talking about?

Bob: You don't remember? We'd play with him in the hall. We'd throw the ball and he'd go get it. Then one day Dad ran over him in the driveway and he was all hurt and dying, but not quite, and you said we have to put him out of his misery, only I couldn't do it because poor Squirt looked so sad and helpless. Then you said you'd do it. Remember? You grabbed that rock and you hit poor Squirt over the head.

Jimmy: Are you telling me that you can't kill this kid because of a fucking dog?

Bob: Well, not just that …

Jimmy: First of all, that wasn't our dog. That was Mrs Pinkton's dog from down the hall. Secondly, Dad didn't kill the damned thing. The cops did. They ran over it about five seconds before they kicked down the door and dragged the old bastard away.

Bob: Really?

Jimmy: Yes! Now think, Bobby. I want you to really think. Why was the old man taken away?

Bob: Awe, c'mon Jimmy. I don't want to do this.

Jimmy: No, you need to learn. Why was the old man taken away?

Bob: Because he made mistakes.

Jimmy: That's right. And what was his biggest mistake?

Bob: He got soft.

Jimmy: And what happens when people go soft?

Bob: They get squished.

Jimmy: Damn straight. They get squished. And we don't want to get squished, do we, Bobby?

Bob: (*mumbles*) No.

Jimmy: Sorry?

Bob: No.

Jimmy: Good, so knock this shit off and finish the job. We shouldn't be here.

Jimmy goes back to the door. Bob puts the pillow over the victim's face again.

Jimmy: Hold up. Someone's coming.

Bob drops the pillow, tries to look innocent. Sally enters, frantic and sobbing. She runs straight past the two brothers and to the bed.

Sally: Nick?! Nick?! I'm here, Nick. Can you hear me? It's Sally. I'm here.

Bob: He can't hear you. I dropped a bedpan earlier. He didn't even flinch.

Sally: Excuse me?

Bob: It wasn't full or anything.

Sally: Who are you?

Bob: I'm Bobby, but most people call me Slow Bob.

Sally: Right. And what are you doing here?

Bob: Well, I was staking out the kid's house and—

Sally: What?

Jimmy: A witness. He's a witness to the accident.

Sally: And what are you? A cop?

Bob: Ha!

Jimmy: Yeah, that's right. (*gives Bob a stern look*) I'm Detective Batton, Miss …?

Sally: Winkle. Sally Winkle. I'm Nick's sister. The doctor said they're not sure if he'll wake up.

Jimmy: Well, these things can be complicated …

Sally: How did this happen?

Bob: Taxi.

Sally: What?

Jimmy: An accident, Ms Winkle. We believe your brother was struck by a car.

Sally: My god. Where?

Bob: Everywhere.

Jimmy: Not far from his house.

Sally: I knew this would happen. I knew it.

Bob: You knew your brother was going to get flattened by a taxi?

Jimmy: What makes you say that Ms Winkle?

Sally: If it wasn't this, it would be something else. (*to victim*) Oh, Nick, I'm so sorry. I should have been there. I should have been there.

Jimmy: Like I said, ma'am. We're pretty sure it was just an accident.

Sally: No, you don't understand. My brother's not the sharpest tool in the shed, detective. Last thing my father said to me before he died was 'Watch him, Sal. He'll get himself into trouble. He ain't as smart as you'.

Sally starts to cry. The brothers are totally disarmed.

Sally: Do you have any family, detective?

Jimmy: Yeah, I got a brother.

Sally: He ever get into trouble?

Jimmy: He's a pain in the arse.

Sally: Nick's always getting into trouble. Damned kid can't think for himself. Always running with the wrong crowd. Bunch of thugs and deadbeats. I try to talk to him. Try to make him see sense. But he has such a thick skull. I tell him, you gotta think, Nick. You gotta think. He just doesn't listen.

Sally sobs. Jimmy tentatively hands her a handkerchief.

Jimmy: Easy. I'm sure it'll be alright.

Sally: No, it won't. I'm all Nicky has. I'm all he's ever had. And I've let him down.

Jimmy: Aye, don't say that. Believe me, I know it ain't easy being someone's keeper. But we can only do our best, eh? Who knows, perhaps Nicky boy's thick skull will save him this time, eh?

Sally gives a wry chuckle. They look to each other and share an unexpected moment of attraction.

Sally: Would you excuse me? I need to talk to the doctor.

Jimmy: Of course.

Sally goes to leave, stops at the door.

Sally: Detective? Can you keep an eye on him while I'm gone?

Jimmy: Yeah. I can do that.

Sally smiles, relieved, then exits. Jimmy watches her go, smitten. Beat. Bob picks up the pillow again.

Bob: Alright, let's do this.

Jimmy: Seriously?

Bob: What?

Jimmy: Put the pillow down.

Bob: What?

Jimmy: Just put it down. We're getting out of here.

Bob: But the kid?

Jimmy: Forget the kid.

Bob: But the boss?

Jimmy: Forget the boss. Just go. Go on. Get.

Jimmy snatches the pillow of Bob, then ushers him out. Jimmy holds the pillow in his hands, stands over the victim, conflicted.

Jimmy: Guess today's your lucky day, kid.

Jimmy drops the pillow and exits. Beat. The sound of the heart monitor fills the room again – beep-beep-beep-beep-beep … flatline.

ENDS

FALLOUT

Cast

Gary, 30s male; doomsday prepper

Dana, 30s female; Gary's wife (also an astrophysicist)

Lucy, 20s female; Gary's lover (and part-time model)

Jason, 20s male; Lucy's lover (and Pilates instructor)

Setting

A home-built fallout shelter

Time

The end of the world!

Synopsis

After surviving the nuclear apocalypse, a smug doomsday prepper tries to convince his wife that she can be happy living in his custom-built fallout shelter ... with his secret lover.

A control console stands centre stage. Red lights flash. A bomb siren blares.

Gary bursts on to stage dragging a reluctant Dana behind him.

Gary: Go, go, go, go! Shut the hatch.

Gary runs to the console and starts pressing buttons.

Dana: Gary, stop.

The siren cuts off, but the lights keep flashing.

Gary: Life support systems online. Generators engaged.

Dana: You promised. No more drills.

Gary: Airlock. Airlock? (*frowns*) Did you shut the hatch?

Dana: You're not listening to me.

Gary: We *really* need to shut the hatch.

Gary dashes off stage.

Dana: Gary, please. If we're going to have meaningful dialogue, you need to stop and engage. You can't keep shutting me out like this.

We hear a heavy metal door slam shut. Gary rushes back in and goes back to the control centre.

Gary: There's no shutting, honey. It's just now's not a good time.

Dana: Then when? When are we gonna do this? After another stupid survival camp? After you waste another hundred grand on this hole in the ground?

Gary: We'll have plenty of time soon.

Dana: No. This obsession. It's changed you. It's changed us. I don't know if I can do this anymore. Gary? (*beat*) Gary?

Gary: I hear you, honey.

Dana: And?

Gary: And you need to get under the table.

Dana: What?

Gary: It's coming. Now!

Gary dives under the console. We hear a huge, end-of-the-world explosion! Everything on stage shakes and rattles. Beat. The lights stop flickering and become constant. Gary jumps out from under the counter, ecstatic!

Gary: Yeah! Did you feel it?! Did you feel it!

Dana: Of course, I fucking felt it! What was it?

Gary: That was it, baby! The big one. Hasta la vista! Sayonara! See ya, wouldn't want to be ya! (*looks at the console display*) Jesus. Look at this. They weren't messing around.

Dana: Who?

Gary: North Korea.

Dana: What?

Gary: Or the Americans. Not that it matters. We're green baby! Nothing can hurt this bad boy! Nothing!

Dana: Gary, what the fuck is going on?

Gary: We're free. Goodbye credit cards. Goodbye mortgage. Goodbye tax man. Goodbye governments!

Dana: Bullshit.

Dana rushes off stage.

Gary: Who's the loser now, suckers! Ha! Goodbye Instagram! Goodbye reality TV. Goodbye Ed Sheeran. I hated you the most.

Dana staggers back on stage, stunned.

Dana: No. This can't be it. I have a house. And a career. And goldfish!

Gary: Don't worry, honey. This isn't the end. Not for us.

Dana: They're dead, Gary. They're all dead.

Gary: (*excited*) I know!

Dana: You knew this was going to happen.

Gary: We built a world of matchsticks. It was always gonna burn.

Dana: But all this time. With the digging and the building and the stockpiling. I thought you were insane. But you saved us. You saved me.

Gary: Of course, honey. I'd never let anything hurt you.

Dana: But I was gone, Gary. I got a new place. I emptied our accounts. I changed the Netflix password.

Gary: Yet, here we are. Together.

Dana: I don't deserve you. I should have listened. I should have supported you.

She starts sobbing.

Gary: Hey, it's okay. We're safe. It's over. Now, it's just you and me …

They share a nice hug. Enter Lucy. She holds a remote control and has a confused expression on her face.

Lucy: Hey, babe. The TVs not working.

Gary: … and Lucy. (*to Lucy*) Yes, dear. The world just ended.

Lucy: Oh. Will it come back on soon?

Gary: Not for a while.

Lucy: But it's the *Survivor* final. That fit guy is killing it.

Dana: Who the fuck is that?

Gary: Honey, you remember Lucy.

Dana: Our wedding planner?

Lucy: Hi, Mrs Wells. Love the dress.

Dana: Why is our wedding planner here?

Lucy: Oh, Gary said it would be cool if we crashed here. You know, until the radiation blows over.

Dana: Really? And how long will that take, Gary? For the 'radiation to blow over'?

Gary: Good question. Lot of variables: payload size, fallout radius …

Dana: Guess.

Gary: I dunno. Ten, twenty years …?

Dana: Twenty years?

Gary: Thirty tops.

Beat.

Dana: Are you fucking her?

Gary: Honey. I think we have bigger things to worry about right now.

Dana: Oh my god. You are. You're fucking her. You're fucking our wedding planner!

Lucy: I model too. Part-time.

Dana: How long?

Gary: Does it matter?

Dana: It matters.

Gary: Five months.

Lucy: Six. New Year's. On the beach.

Gary: Oh, yeah. But that's not important right now.

Dana: She was here first.

Beat.

Gary: Honey.

Dana: No. You figured out the world was going to end, and you went and got her. Then you got me. What was I? An afterthought?

Gary: Of course not. It's just geographically it made more sense to get her first.

Dana: Fuck geography! I'm your wife!

Gary: You're overreacting.

Dana: I was at my parents' house, Gary. With my parents. You didn't bring them.

Gary: Now you're being hysterical.

Lucy: You should cut him some slack, Mrs Wells. I mean, without Gary we'd all be dead. And homeless.

Dana: Did she say homeless *after* dead?

Lucy: But look at this place. Gary's thought of everything. We've got food. Water. Chocolate. Scrabble. He's kind of a genius.

Dana: Genius? Genius! Tell me, genius: how many tampons did you pack for our twenty years underground? (*Gary's stumped*) Yeah, real fucking Einstein. How do you think this is gonna work? What are we gonna do down here? Play Scrabble all day and have threesomes all night?

Gary: (*intrigued*) Is that what *you* want to do?

Dana: You son of a bitch.

Gary: Honey. Please. We need to be practical about this. We've got a very important job ahead of us.

Dana: What job?

Gary: To secure the survival of our species.

Dana: (*disbelief*) Fuck off.

Gary: Don't worry. I've done the math. If we have six kids in the first ten years, then at least three more after that, we'll have a viable seed population for our return to the surface.

Lucy: Oh, I love kids! I babysit my nieces all the time. They're probably dead now …

Dana: I should have left. I should have got that boob job. Should have fucked that Uber driver. I could have died happy.

Gary: I know. It sounds like a lot. But with your hips …

Dana: What the fuck does that mean?

Gary: It means you have great hips! Wide. Strong. That's why I married you.

Dana: You married me for my hips?!

Gary: You're a pretty good cook too.

Dana: I'm an astrophysicist, Gary! I have three degrees!

Gary: Yes, well, star signs aren't gonna help us now, are they? No, we need to be strategic. We all have a role to play.

Dana: And my role is to cook and have babies?

Gary: Now you're getting it.

Dana: And your role?

Gary: To maintain the bunker and provide for the family.

Dana: Right. So, what the fuck is Malibu Barbie bringing to the table?

They look over to Lucy. She's bent over to pick something up off the floor. They stare at her arse.

Gary: Well, she has *other* skills …

Dana: Oh my god. I can't do this. I can't …

Gary: Of course, you can. You're a strong, independent woman. Who has no choice.

Dana: No. Fuck that. Open the door.

Gary: I can't do that.

Dana: Open the fucking door!

Gary: If I do, we all die. You don't want that.

Dana: You're right. I don't want us all to die. I just want you to die.

She reaches under the console desk and pulls out a gun.

Gary: Honey …

Dana: Oh, look. It's the gun I asked you not to buy. In the bunker I asked you not to build. In the life I asked you not to destroy!

Gary: C'mon. The North Koreans did that one …

Lucy: Or the Americans …

Dana: I might be stuck in this bunker, but I'm not gonna be stuck with you.

Gary: Honey. You can't kill me.

Dana: I've course I can. I'm a strong independent woman.

Gary: But you need me. I'm the only one who knows how this stuff works.

Dana: I'll figure it out.

Lucy: Oh, it's not hard. (*points to the console*) Filtration system. Generator. CO_2 levels.

Dana: You did the drills?

Lucy: They were kinda hot.

Dana: Gross. Though it does make genius boy here rather redundant.

Gary: Honey. I saved you.

Dana: You put me in a cage.

Gary: To save the world!

Dana: You don't want to save the world. You want to be the centre of it.

Gary: Please. Think about this. I'm the last man alive. If you kill me, that's it. Our entire species will cease to exist! Is that what you want? As a scientist?

She wavers above him but can't do it.

Dana: God damn it! This is such bullshit! I was a good person. So why? Why couldn't I die like everyone else? Why do I have to spend the rest of my miserable life trapped in this shithole of a bunker … with you …? (*sobs*)

Lucy: And me.

Dana: And her (*sobs harder*) …

Lucy: And Jason.

Dana: And Jason. (*stops sobbing*) Wait. Who?

Enter Jason. He's hot and charming – not at all like Gary.

Jason: Hey, babe. The TV's still broken.

Lucy: Yeah, the world just ended.

Jason: Oh. Will it come back on soon?

Lucy: Apparently not …

Gary: Who the fuck is this?

Lucy: Oh, honey. You remember Jason. My Pilates instructor.

Gary: Who?

Jason: You must be Gary. Great place. Appreciate you letting us crash.

Gary: Crash? But you're not … I was … we …

Dana: Last man alive, huh? (*admiring Jason*) Hi, I'm Dana.

Jason: G'day. Looks like we're gonna be here a while. Don't know how we're gonna pass the time.

Dana: Oh, I'm sure we'll think of something. (*beat*) Do you like Scrabble?

ENDS

THE TRUTH ABOUT MUM AND DAD

Cast

Rachel, 30s female; professional and uptight

Jason, 20s male; Rachael's carefree brother

Setting

A cafe

Time

Saturday afternoon

Synopsis

After discovering their Dad's ute parked outside a brothel, two siblings come together to discuss the ins and outs of their parent's sex life.

Rachael sits alone at a cafe table. She's trying to discreetly peer through a pair of binoculars at something offstage. Jason enters unseen. He sees Rachael all alone and approaches in mock rage.

Jason: You bitch!

Rachael: (*confused*) Hey?

Jason: Did you think I wouldn't find out?

Rachael: What?

Jason: I put cameras around the house, Rach. I saw everything.

Rachael: Really? You're gonna do this? Now?

Jason: I thought you loved me.

Rachael: Jason. Sit down.

Jason: And with Jerry? Jerry!? He's like a brother to me.

Rachael: Jase.

Jason: When did it start? Before the salsa lessons? After? I knew you couldn't resist a man who can dance.

Rachael: I said sit down! (*she drags him into a chair*) What the fuck is wrong with you?

Jason: (*laughs*) Dude. You should see your face. Classic.

Rachael: You're such a dick.

Jason: A funny dick.

Rachael: Everyone is looking at us.

Jason: I know. Look at that guy. He's trying to take sneaky pics. (*smiles and waves*)

Rachael: You need to grow up.

Jason: C'mon. You used to love this shit. Remember the long-lost sibling routine we pulled at school? The squabbling newly-weds at that restaurant? Amnesia girl at the psychic convention?

Rachael: Yeah. Hilarious.

Jason: Jesus. What's your problem? Is this about David?

Rachael: No.

Jason: Rach, it's been a year. You got to let it go.

Rachael: Don't tell me what to do.

Jason: C'mon. I want my sis back? Remember her? Yay tall. Wicked smile. Does palm farts in crowded elevators. She was fun.

Rachael: Don't. Okay? Just, don't.

Jason: So, what's the deal? What's wrong with the joint near my place?

Rachael: There's something you need to see.

Jason: God. It's not the coffee, is it? Sis, don't care what the hipsters say. Coffee isn't game. It doesn't need to be hunted.

Rachael: Look. Over there.

She hands him the binoculars. He peers through.

Jason: Sin-sations. A strip club. You brought me to see a strip club?

Rachael: It's not a strip club. It's a …

Jason: What?

Rachael: You know. A place men go to …

Jason: To what?

Rachael: To pay … for … (*Jason shrugs, confused*) Sex, Jason! It's a place men go to pay for sex.

Jason: Oh. A brothel. You brought me to see a brothel? (*too loud*) She brought me to see a brothel!

Rachael: Look at the car. Out front.

Jason: Looks like Dad's old ute.

Rachael: It is Dad's old ute.

Jason: Huh. Crazy.

Rachael: Really? 'Crazy'? That's all you can say? Jason! I think Dad's in there. I think he's diddling with prostitutes.

Jason: (*amused*) Diddling.

Rachael: I'm serious.

Jason: He's probably visiting someone nearby.

Rachael: Since when does Dad do social calls?

Jason: He goes to the pub with his mates.

Rachael: This isn't the RSL, Jason! It's a brothel!

Jason: Did you actually see him go inside?

Rachael: Well. No. But I called. Like twenty minutes ago. He said he was at the farmer's market. Across town. He was lying.

Jason: Was he out of breath?

Rachael: Jason! Dad's sleeping with prostitutes!

Jason: You don't know that.

Rachael: How could he? How could he do that to Mum? I thought they were solid. Mum's gonna be humiliated.

Jason: Give her a little credit.

Rachael: What's that supposed to mean?

Jason: Who knows? Maybe she knows. Maybe she's cool with it.

Rachael: Cool with it! Mum? She can't even say 'sex' without blushing. It's like she's allergic. Her eye gets all twitchy. She gets that stutter. Remember when she gave us the talk? It was like getting sex advice from Porky Pig. (*Porky Pig impersonation*) 'Now it's, er, p-p-perfectly normal for the, er, for the, er, p-p-penis to become e-e-erect.'

Jason: Maybe they decided to spice things up.

Rachael: Oh, that's what this is. Just Mum and Dad 'spicing things up'.

Jason: Why not? They lived through the sixties. Swinging, swapping, role-playing. They invented that stuff.

Rachael: Mum and Dad are not swingers! Mum's a prude, for god's sake.

Jason: Mum is no prude. Believe me.

Rachael: What?

Jason: Let's just say I've seen things.

Rachael: What things?

Jason: Things no son should see.

Rachael: Like?

Jason: You remember Dad's old recliner?

Rachael: Yeah.

Jason: You know why he threw it away?

Rachael: Dog jumped on it. Broke the lever thing.

Jason: Wasn't the dog. It was Mum. And Dad. They were … on it …

Rachael: In the living room?

Jason: On a Sunday afternoon.

Rachael: Fuck off.

Jason: They thought I was at work. I came out of my room and *BAM* there it was. Dad's arse. Bouncing.

Rachael: Fuck me.

Beat.

Jason: Still, it's not as bad as the whole pool thing.

Rachael: What pool thing?

Jason: You ever wondered why Dad maintains a swimming pool they never use?

Rachael: Habit?

Jason: I thought so too. Turns out they do use it. A lot.

Rachael: Mum hates swimming. She thinks the chlorine will make her bald.

Jason: That's why she wears a swimming cap. That's all she wears.

Rachael: Mum skinny-dips?

Jason: Dad too. They slip out the back, toss their clothes and … splash around.

Rachael: They have sex in the pool?

Jason: Oh yeah. You ever seen *Show Girls*? It's like that. Mum thrashes her arms. Her body flips and flops. Actually, it's more like *Jaws* now I think about it …

Rachael: Still, that doesn't mean Mum's okay with this.

Jason: Yeah? Then what about the French onion dip?

Rachael: Am I supposed to know what that means?

Jason: Okay, so, a few months back I had some mates around to watch a game. You know, Benny, Craig. The usual crew. Anyway, I raid the kitchen for supplies: beer, chips, dip, whatever. So, I'm hunting through the pantry and I find two packets of rice crackers and two types of dip. One French onion, the other plain guacamole.

Rachael: So?

Jason: So, I don't like French onion. So, I left it. Just took the rice crackers and the guacamole.

Rachael: What the fuck are you talking about?

Jason: Two days later I go back, and the French onion was gone.

Rachael: And?

Jason: Where did it go, Rach?

Rachael: I dunno? They ate it?

Jason: Yes. But with what? I took the rice crackers. They didn't have no corn chips. So, what did they eat it with?

Rachael: Celery?

Jason: Yes. If by celery you mean ... (*nods knowingly to his crotch*)

Rachael: (*confused*) What?

Jason: You know. They must have dipped something else instead ... (*nods to his crotch again*)

Rachael: Oh, c'mon!

Jason: What else could it have been!

Rachael: Seriously? Some dip goes missing and you assume they're having kinky food sex?

Jason: After the recliner and the pool, I'm not ruling anything out.

Rachael: Fuck. I knew you'd do this. I call you for help, and what do you do? Dick around. Everything's just a fucking joke to you.

Jason: French onion dick is no joke, sis.

Beat.

Rachael: This is why you don't have serious relationships.

Jason: Please. I've had plenty.

Rachael: Name one.

Jason: Cassie was serious.

Rachael: You dated for like four months.

Jason: Yeah. But it was serious. Met her family and everything.

Rachael: You slept with her sister! That's not 'meeting the family'!

Jason: It wasn't her sister. It was her cousin.

Rachael: Oh, excuse me! Sister. Cousin. Neighbour. Hooker. What the difference? You. Dad. David. You're all a bunch of dicks.

Jason: Rach …

Rachael: No. It's pathetic. It's like you don't know. You just piss it away. And for what? To diddle your little dandys in something new for a day!

Jason: Rach …

Rachael: It's such bullshit. I swore I'd never let that happen. But it's just what you bastards do. You fuck around. All of you. Even Dad's over there getting it on with god knows what—

Jason: Rachael! Dad's not sleeping with prostitutes.

Beat.

Rachael: But that's his ute …

Jason: That was his ute. He sold it. Like two months ago. Which is something you'd know if you came home once in a while.

Rachael: So, he's not …?

Jason: Of course not. It's Dad.

Rachael: And you knew this? The whole time? Jason! What the fuck!? Why would you do that?

Jason: It was funny.

Rachael: Funny!? Funny!?

Jason: Yeah. It's hilarious. And if you weren't so wrapped up in your own head, you'd think so too. C'mon. Dad? Doing prostitutes? The old bugger won't switch brands of soap and you think he's over here taste testing hookers on the weekends?

Beat.

Rachael: Oh my god. I thought Dad was sleeping with hookers.

Jason: Diddling, actually.

Rachael: I thought he was cheating on Mum.

Jason: Like a regular Tiger Woods.

Rachael: I thought … (*beat*) Jesus. I'm an idiot.

Jason: Yes. Yes, you are.

Rachael: And you're a prick.

Jason: A funny prick.

Rachael: So, all that stuff about Mum and Dad. That was bullshit, right?

Jason: I wish. Seriously. They are kinky as. The other day Mum got a package. It was vibrating—

Rachael: God. Please. Stop. Just stop.

Beat. Rachael gets up to leave.

Jason: Where you going?

Rachael: See Mum and Dad. Think I owe them a visit.

Jason: Seriously? It took me like forty minutes to get here. At least buy me a coffee.

Rachael: Yeah. Can't do that.

Jason: Why not?

Rachael: Because you're a bastard!

Jason: (*confused*) What?

Rachael: (*stands up and yells*) I said, you're a bastard! You're never there, Jason! Not for our anniversary. Not for my birthday. Not for my mother's birthday. But Jerry. He's there. In our bed. In our car. On our kitchen bench. I've let him put things in places you could only dream of. And I loved it. (*slaps him across the face*) Don't bother coming home. (*whispers*) Should see your face. Classic.

Rachael exits, big smile on her face.

Jason: Good to have you back. Bitch.

ENDS

THE UNEXPECTED

Cast

Lisa, 40s female; a mother of one (expectant mother of two)

Jeannie, 17 female; daughter of two (expectant mother of one)

Robert, 40s male; Lisa's husband and Jeannie's father

Setting

Family dining room

Time

Evening

Synopsis

A mother and her teenage daughter discover they both have some very unexpected news – they're both expecting!

Lisa, wearing an apron over a beautiful evening gown, sits at a romantic table for two. She rehearses for a big conversation that's yet to happen.

Lisa: Honey, look. I know you don't like surprises but … Honey. Baby. I know we've been talking about scaling back but … Honey! C'mon down! Have I got some news for you! … No! Stupid! … Honey. Do you love me?

Lisa's phone rings and she answers.

Lisa: Hey! Where are you? Where? Did you get my messages? Yes, tonight. No, it can't wait! She's at the movies. Yes, with 'Super Meat Boy'. I told you this. I did. Last night. And this morning. It doesn't matter. When will you be home? Cos I've got a surprise. Of course it's a good one. No. Because it's a surprise. Look, just get home. Okay? Soon as you can. Okay. See you soon.

A beat as she takes in the set dinner table. Offstage, an oven DINGS. She checks her reflection in a spoon, then exits.

Jeannie enters, pauses when she sees the dinner scene.

Jeannie: Mum? Dad?

Lisa returns.

Lisa: Hey, that was fast! I thought— Oh, darling. What are you doing home?

Jeannie: I live here. Remember?

Lisa: I thought you were going to the movies.

Jeannie: I was.

Lisa: So?

Jeannie: So, what?

Lisa: So, what are you doing here?

Jeannie: What? I can't come home when I feel like it?

Lisa: Of course. I just wasn't expecting you.

Jeannie: Obviously. What's going on?

Lisa: Nothing. I'm just putting together a nice meal for your father. What do you think?

Jeannie: I think you're acting weird.

Lisa: How so?

Jeannie: You're using the fancy cutlery for starters.

Lisa: What fancy cutlery?

Jeannie: This stuff. We only use this at Christmas. Or when Dad's creepy boss comes round. Shit. He's not here is he?

Lisa: No. And don't use that word. You sound uncouth.

Jeannie: Did you and Dad have another fight?

Lisa: You say that like we always fight.

Jeannie: You do.

Lisa: We do not. We fight an appropriate amount.

Jeannie: More than appropriate lately.

Lisa: Yes. Well, things have been a little tense. Your father's been busy at work and I … well, I've been going through some things of my own. But it's nothing for you to worry about.

Jeannie: Is that why you're wearing heels? And lipstick? And that dress? Oh god. I just realised what this is. This is date night!

Lisa: What?

Jeannie: Date night. You guys are gonna … gross!

Lisa: Oh, Jeannie. Stop it.

Jeannie: It'll be the laundry scene all over again.

Lisa: I thought we agreed to not speak about that. Besides, that's what you get when you skip school and decide to creep around the house all day.

Jeannie: But why on the washing machine, Mum? I use that.

Lisa: You do not. And stop being silly. Tonight's not like that. I told you. Your father and I are having a nice meal. It's not often we get the house to ourselves. Which is why you have to skedaddle.

Jeannie: Hey?

Lisa: That's right. Off you go.

Jeannie: You're kicking me out?

Lisa: Yep.

Jeannie: Where am I supposed to go?

Lisa: I'm sure Grandma would love a visit. Or Uncle Phil. They're always saying they don't see enough of you.

Jeannie: They live on the other side of town.

Lisa: I'll give you money for a taxi.

Jeannie: Seriously? That's gonna cost like fifty bucks. I'm flat out getting fifteen out of you for a movie ticket.

Lisa: Then I guess it's your lucky night.

Jeannie: I don't want to go to Grandma's.

Lisa: And I didn't want to sit through three hours of *Batman* with your father. But what are you gonna do?

Jeannie: Mum, I'm serious. I want to stay home tonight.

Lisa: Why? Did you and Devon have a tiff? Is that why you're home?

Jeannie: No. Well, yes. But that's not why I came home.

Lisa: You've lost me.

Jeannie: I'm just not feeling well.

Lisa: Oh, honey. Why didn't you say so? What's the matter? Is it cramps?

Jeannie: It's not cramps, Mum.

Lisa: Are you hot? Might be that flu that's going round.

Jeannie: I think it's more a belly thing?

Lisa: What makes you say that?

Jeannie: I puked all over Devon's car.

Lisa: Oh, honey. Are you okay?

Jeannie: Yeah. But he was pissed. Then we fought.

Lisa: Yes. Well, puke doesn't bring out the best in people. Will you be alright?

Jeannie: Yeah. I just wanted to come home and, you know, regather.

Lisa: Of course, honey. Of course. (*she hugs Jeannie*) Okay, now run along.

Jeannie: Mum!

Lisa: What? You said you were fine.

Jeannie: Yeah, but there's something else I want to talk about. Before Dad gets home.

Lisa: Look. Jeannie. I know Devon is a big deal right now. I get it. I had a boyfriend at your age. Everything feels so important. But believe me, it'll be fine. He'll get over the puke.

Jeannie: Yeah, I know. But—

Lisa: Good. So off you go.

Jeannie: Why do you always do this?

Lisa: What?

Jeannie: This. You dismiss me.

Lisa: I don't dismiss you.

Jeannie: You do. All the time.

Lisa: You're being silly.

Jeannie: That's exactly what I'm talking about!

Lisa: I'm not dismissing you. I'm … postponing you.

Jeannie: But this is important.

Lisa: So is this dinner.

Jeannie: You have dinner with Dad every night!

Lisa: Yes. But tonight we have things to discuss.

Jeannie: You're not listening to me!

Lisa: I'm listening just fine. You don't seem to be hearing my response.

Jeannie: God. I'm so sick of you doing this! You don't listen.

Jeannie	Lisa
If you could just pay attention for ten seconds instead of fobbing me off, you'd realise I have something important to say. But no. You can't do that. It's always, 'Not now, honey'. Or 'Later honey'. Or 'I'm in the middle of something now, honey'. Well this can't wait. I need to talk about this. I need you to listen to me. Mum, please, stop. Mum, please. Listen to me. Mum! Why aren't you listening! Mum …	I listen. I'm listening. But I can't drop everything every time you and Devon have a fight. There are other things happening in the world, Jeannie. Other people! I have needs too. I need time to figure things out. I don't feel like I'm asking for much. I need to talk to your father. There are things that need to be said. Are you hearing me? Do you know what I'm trying to say? Jeannie …

Jeannie	Lisa
I'm pregnant!	I'm pregnant!
(*beat*)	(*beat*)
What!?	What!?
(*beat*)	(*beat*)
But you're too old!	But you're too young!
(*beat*)	(*beat*)
What does that mean!?	What does that mean!?

Lisa: Hang on. What do you mean 'you're pregnant'?

Jeannie: What do you mean 'what do I mean'? I'm pregnant. I don't know how else to say it.

Lisa: But you can't be?

Jeannie: Then it's a miracle.

Lisa: But when? How?

Jeannie: Well, Devon and I drove up to the lake and—

Lisa: I don't mean *how*? I know *how*? I mean *how*? How could you let this happen, Jeannie? You know better than this. What have I always told you?

Jeannie: To use my head and to only do what felt right.

Lisa: That's right.

Jeannie: It felt right, Mum.

Lisa: You're seventeen years old!

Jeannie: I know!

Lisa: This is Devon's fault. Did he pressure you? I know boys can be … insistent.

Jeannie: It's not Devon's fault, Mum. But we both wanted it. We just didn't think …

Lisa: Your father was right. He's like a slimy little piece of processed meat.

Jeannie: Mum!

Lisa: Jeannie. You're pregnant!

Jeannie: I know! So are you.

Lisa: I know!

Jeannie: So why are you yelling at me?

Lisa: I don't know! It feels right!

Jeannie: Well stop it. I'm freaking out here. I can't have a kid. I'm not even sure I want a kid. I know Devon doesn't. You should have seen his face when I told him. He just sat there. Staring. He couldn't even look at me. That's when I puked. Right there in the car. He was like, 'Watch the seats, man! I just had these cleaned!' He was totally flipping out. And now you're flipping out. And later Dad's gonna flip out. And I don't know what to do. What am I supposed to do!

Jeannie bursts into tears.

Lisa: Oh, hey. Honey. I'm sorry. Come here. I'm sorry. Hey, it's okay. It's gonna be okay. I just … you caught me off guard. I've been so worried about telling your father about me that I … Hey, it's gonna be okay. Okay? I know. It's terrifying. I'm scared too. But we'll figure this out. Everything's gonna be alright. I promise. Everything will be fine.

Lisa hugs Jeannie. Beat.

Jeannie: I've ruined everything.

Lisa: No one has ruined anything.

Jeannie: Devon hates me.

Lisa: He doesn't. He's shitting his pants right now, but he doesn't hate you. God, this is my fault. You're right. I haven't been listening. I've been so wrapped up in my own head. I swore I'd do better than this.

Jeannie: Mum, I didn't have sex with Devon because of you. I did it because he's hot.

Lisa: Still. I've been totally freaking out about this. I've been trying to figure out how to tell your father. He's been talking about making changes. Cutting back at work. Taking some time for himself. We were so young when we had you. There were a lot of things we never got to do. Now along comes another surprise. Or two.

Jeannie: I'm sorry, Mum.

Lisa: No, that's not what I meant. I just wasn't expecting this. Not with me. Not again. And certainly not with you.

Jeannie: So you're not pissed?

Lisa: I'm furious. But I love you. And we'll get through this. Together. (*beat*) You want to know something funny?

Jeannie: What?

Lisa: The day I told your father I was pregnant with you, I puked all over his car too.

Jeannie: Really?

Lisa: Yep. His little Datsun. There were chunks of gurge everywhere. On the seats. On the dash. In the ashtray. We found those about two weeks later.

Jeannie: How'd he take it?

Lisa: He freaked. We were young. He thought his life was over.

Jeannie: What changed?

Lisa: Time. He just needed some time to get his head around things. That's the funny thing about men. They're idiots. All they want to do is play with their cars and comic books. Yet they have the uncanny knack of stepping up when they need to. The good ones anyway.

Jeannie: You think Devon will step up?

Lisa: Dunno. Maybe. Either way you've got me. And your father.

Jeannie: Dad's gonna freak.

Lisa: It's gonna be an interesting conversation, that's for sure.

Jeannie: But he'll come around, right? He'll just need some time.

Lisa: And beer. Lots and lots of beer.

Beat.

Jeannie: Mum?

Lisa: Yeah?

Jeannie: You and Dad ... it wasn't on the washing machine, was it?

Lisa: Timing fits. And it was a good angle.

Jeannie: Oh, god!

Lisa: C'mon. He'll be home soon.

Jeannie: Right. I'll leave you to it then.

Lisa: Like hell. I'm not doing this by myself. Set a place. Dinner for two just became a family affair.

Jeannie: You know you don't need this, right? The dinner. The dress. You can talk to Dad. He loves you. He'll listen.

Lisa: I know. I guess I just needed a reminder. Stay here. I'm gonna change out of this stupid dress.

Robert charges in, excited. He's carrying a box full of office supplies.

Robert: Honey! Guess what?! I did it! I finally did it! I quit my job!

ENDS

SEXY BETH'S GIANT DILDO COLLECTION

Cast

Beth, 20s female; not a dildo collector

Dale, 20s male; Beth's boyfriend

Phillip, 50s male; Beth's father

Setting

A newly rented apartment

Time

A Sunday afternoon

Synopsis

Having the sex talk is never easy – especially with your new girlfriend's oversharing and sexually adventurous father.

A house moving scene: cardboard boxes, discarded packing paper, general disorder. Beth enters carrying a box. She starts unpacking it but seems overwhelmed by the chaos of the move.

Phillip enters. He's carrying a huge box with bold letters on the side: 'SEXY BETH'S GIANT DILDO COLLECTION'.

Phillip: Another box, dear.

Beth: Great. Just chuck it anywhere.

Phillip places the box centre stage.

Phillip: All good in here?

Beth: Yeah. Just trying to figure out where to start.

Phillip: Need a hand?

Beth: Nah. I got it.

Phillip: Right. Well, I guess I'll just keep helping Dale then.

Beth: Thanks, Dad. Appreciate it.

Phillip exits. Dale enters with more boxes.

Dale: Jesus. Next time we're taking the place on the ground floor. Stairs are killing me.

Beth: Thought you liked the stairs. Thought they were 'Old school cool'.

Dale: Babe, there's old school, then there's old school. Lifting that fridge is gonna be a pain in the arse.

Beth: Don't worry. Dad's here.

Dale: He is. Nice of him to turn up like that. Unannounced.

Beth: Stop it. He wants to help.

Dale: How? By browbeating me all day?

Beth: He's not browbeating you.

Dale: He is. He's like that flaming eye from *Lord of the Rings*. Always watching.

Beth: You're the new guy. It's his job to suss you out.

Dale: Still, the way he looks at me. You know he brought his own box cutter? Like, a personalised one. Who carries around a personalised box cutter?

Beth: Where'd we get all this crap?

Dale: That's how it works, Babe. Throw two people together and *BAM* – spontaneous stuff.

Beth: It's not gonna fit.

Dale: Sure it is. Put up some shelves. Hang a few hooks. We'll be right. (*beat*) What's the matter?

Beth: Nothing.

Dale: Babe.

Beth: It's just, this is really happening.

Dale: Damn right it is. This is it. Game on! (*beat*) You're not having second thoughts?

Beth: What? No. It's just, this is the start. Of everything. You. Me. Us. This place. I just need things to go smooth. I don't want any hiccups.

Dale: Babe, chill. We totally got this. Besides, I've never had hiccups a day in my life.

Beth: Not once?

Dale: Well, yeah. I was just trying to …

Beth: (*laughing*) Shut up.

They kiss. A nice moment. Then Beth spots the giant dildo box.

Beth: What the hell is that?

Dale: What?

Beth: That.

Dale: Oh, shit. Totally forgot about that.

Beth: What do you mean 'you forgot'?

Dale: It was a joke.

Beth: You wrote that?

Dale: I thought you'd laugh.

Beth: Dale! What the fuck?!

Dale: What? You've been stressing all day. I wanted to lighten the mood.

Beth: Please tell me my father didn't see that.

Dale: He might have.

Beth: Might have?

Dale: He's been carrying boxes all day.

Beth: Did he carry this one?

Dale: I dunno.

Beth: Did you?

Dale: Maybe.

Beth: Dale!

Dale: There are a lot of boxes!

Beth: Great. Just great.

Dale: Babe. Relax. He probably didn't even notice.

Beth: Look at it. It says 'Sexy Beth's Giant Dildo Collection' right there! You'd have to be Mr Fucking Magoo to miss that!

Dale: You're overreacting.

Beth: Dale. My father now thinks I own a box of giant sex toys.

Dale: (*chuckles*) Huh.

Beth: What?

Dale: Oh, it's just, I was thinking the collection was giant. Not the actual …

Beth: Not the point! I don't want my father thinking I'm some sort of sick sexual deviant.

Dale: (*playfully grabs her*) If only he knew …

Beth: (*she pushes him away*) This isn't a joke.

Dale: Babe, relax. The box is full of towels.

Beth: So? He doesn't know that.

Dale: So, we'll just explain.

Beth: Oh, we'll just explain. Of course. How silly of me. (*to an imaginary Phillip*). Hey, Dad. You know that giant box of dildos you carried in? Don't worry. I'm not really an avid collector of novelty-sized sex toys. My new boyfriend just likes to pretend I am. He likes to humiliate me in front of the people I love. I know, hilarious, right? And you said I should have married that doctor.

Dale: I wasn't trying to humiliate you.

Beth: Well you have.

Dale: I didn't know your dad was gonna rock up.

Beth: But he did. Don't you see? He's coming around. He sees that you're important to me. That you're not like all the other guys.

Dale: What other guys?

Beth: Really? That's what you took from that?

Dale: How many we talking?

Beth: Focus. We need to fix this.

Dale: Look. If it's bothering you, we can put it in the other room.

Beth: And what? Just pretend nothing happened?

Dale: It worked for the Clintons.

Beth: No, it didn't!

Dale: No, it didn't …

Beth: Things have always been good between me and Dad. Easy. I don't want things to get weird.

Dale: So, just add it to the list.

Beth: What list?

Dale: The list. Of 'awkward shit that happens, that families never talk about'.

Beth: What?

Dale: You know. Embarrassing stuff. Like when I was fifteen and Mum caught me whacking it to one of her Avon catalogues.

Beth: Your mother caught you masturbating?

Dale: I was alone. There was nothing good on TV.

Beth: So, the next logical step was to whip it out and shake it?

Dale: I was fifteen. Of course, it was.

Beth: Jesus …

Dale: I know. We just stood there. Her with a handful of groceries. Me with a handful … (*beat*) But I was lucky. She put it on the list. Never said a word about it.

Beth: Never?

Dale: That's the beauty of the list. You just pretend. My family do it all the time. We pretend my mother never caught me flogging it. We pretend my parents don't hump under the Christmas tree each year. We pretend my brother didn't meet his wife in rehab.

Beth: That doesn't sound very healthy.

Dale: You kidding? Healthiest thing we do.

Beth: Then your family has issues.

Dale: And yours doesn't?

Beth: Not like that.

Dale: Bullshit. Every family has a list.

Beth: No. Just the freaky ones.

Dale: C'mon. So, you never caught your parents doing it?

Beth: No.

Dale: Never found your brother's dirty magazines?

Beth: No.

Dale: Never made an appointment at a 'massage parlour' only to rock up and find your dad sitting in the waiting room?

Beth: No. We're not like that. We're civilised.

Dale: Oh, excuse me.

Beth: You know what I mean. We don't do that kind of thing.

Dale: Oh my god. You're a prude.

Beth: I am not a prude.

Dale: You are. Sure, you might be an insatiable animal in the sack, but out here, in the cold light of day, you're nothing but a big fat juicy prude.

Beth: I'm not a prude. I'm … discreet. Which is why we need to fix this.

Dale: Look. He seems like a reasonable guy. Let's just tell him the truth. He might think it's funny.

Beth: You think?

Dale: I think it's funny.

Beth: Yes, but you come from a family of sex offenders.

Dale: Never heard you complain …

Dale grabs Beth playfully. She pushes him away.

Beth: I can't.

Dale: Can't what?

Beth: Talk to him. We don't do that.

Dale: You don't talk?

Beth: No. Sex.

Dale: You don't sex?

Beth: We don't talk about it!

Dale: Ever?

Beth: Not with my parents.

Dale: Then how did you have 'the talk'?

Beth: Didn't.

Dale: Then how did you learn about the birds and the bees?

Beth: Normal way. Internet.

Dale: So that's why you slap me and call me bitch during sex?

Beth: You have to do it.

Dale: Babe, I don't mind it a bit rough. But you don't *have* to do it …

Beth: No. *You* have to do it. You have to talk to Dad.

Dale: Me?

Beth: It was your joke!

Dale: I hardly know the guy.

Beth: It'll help you bond.

Dale: Seriously? This is how you want us to bond?

Beth: Look. You and your feral family might be able to live with a list of weird unspeakable shit hanging over your heads. But I can't. I don't want my dad picturing me doing that. (*points to the box*). It's weird.

Dale: It's not that weird.

Beth: It's weird! Babe. Please. This is our first day in this place. I don't want it marred by some stupid masturbatory misunderstanding with my father.

Beat.

Dale: Fine. I'll talk to him. But if he pulls out that box cutter, I'm bailing.

Phillip enters with more boxes.

Phillip: Alright. Just the fridge to go. (*off the tension*) Everything alright?

Beth: Yeah. All good. Actually, I need a break. How about I pop out and grab some coffees?

Phillip: Sounds good. I'll come.

Beth: No. You stay. With Dale. Chat. I won't be long.

Phillip: You sure?

Beth: Positive.

Phillip: (*confused*) Okay …?

Beth exits, gesturing for Dale to fix the situation. Beat as Phillip and Dale stand awkwardly, the box between them.

Dale: Good of you to help us out today.

Phillip: Not a problem. Moving always gets a little crazy. Thought you could use an extra pair of hands.

Dale: Totally. (*beat*) Actually, speaking of crazy, Mr Phillips—

Phillip: Phil.

Dale: Sorry?

Phillip: Call me Phil.

Dale: Right. (*beat*) Wait, Phil Phillips? (*beat*) Okay. Phil. Look. I know things between Beth and I have moved fast …

Phillip: Uh-huh …?

Dale: Well, I just want you to know I only have her best interests at heart.

Phillip: Good of you to say.

Dale: Yeah. So, with that in mind. The box …

Phillip: Box?

Dale: Yeah. The box …

Phillip: Oh. The box.

Dale: Yeah. Beth's a little embarrassed. And angry. Actually, she's really angry. So, I just wanted to—

Phillip: Dale. It's okay.

Dale: It is?

Phillip: You don't have to explain.

Dale: I don't?

Phillip: Course not. We're all adults. Nothing to be embarrassed about.

Dale: That's kinda what I'm getting at. See the box is full of—

Phillip: You know how long I've been married, Dale? Thirty-two years.

Dale: Really?

Phillip: Hasn't always been easy. Lot of ups and downs. Lot of battles. You know what gets us through?

Dale: Booze?

Phillip: Honesty.

Dale: Right …

Phillip: Beth's mother and I have always been honest. About everything. Our goals. Our dreams. Our … desires.

Dale: Desires?

Phillip: That's what I see here, Dale. (*taps the box*) Honesty. You and Beth are obviously open with one another. Sexually. I admire that.

Dale: You do?

Phillip: You know where I met my wife, Dale?

Dale: Uni?

Phillip: Bankstown Players.

Dale: Bankstown Players? What's that? Amateur theatre?

Phillip: Swingers club.

Dale: What club!?

Phillip: I'll never forget it. First time I laid eyes on her, she was being spit roasted by two footballers and a chartered accountant named Clive.

Dale: Fuck me!

Phillip: It was the most erotic thing I have ever seen. She was so uninhibited. So primal. So … flexible.

Dale: (*calling out*) Beth …?

Phillip: Those first years were unbelievable. Make Woodstock look like a children's birthday party. Swinging. Swapping. Spanking. Bondage. S&M. Toys. Lot of toys. (*taps the box*) Tell me, Dale; have you ever gifted a woman a forty-eight-hour orgasm?

Dale: Is that physically possible?

Phillip: Of course, it is. Tickle here. Bit of pressure there. You'd be amazed what the human body can do. I once saw a flight attendant blow a gum bubble so big, they had to scrape it off the ceiling. (*beat*) She wasn't using her mouth.

Dale: Oh. My. God.

Phillip: That reminds me. You know how I got this scar?

Dale: Please say shaving …

Phillip: Rope burn. This is what fourteen hours tied to a rocking horse in a Parramatta love den will get you. Pro tip: (*pulls out a box cutter*) always carry a box cutter. Always. Oh, and if you ever hire a Spanish dominatrix, don't use 'estrico' as your safe word. Things can get tight.

Dale: I will never forget that.

Phillip: You know, it's funny. After the sixties, we thought the world was gonna change. Thought it would loosen up. Shed its inhibitions. Shake its taboos. But it didn't. No, once the green haze wore off everyone just buttoned up and carried on. Don't get me wrong. There's a lot of sex around these days. Can't turn on the TV or drive by a billboard without a pair of tits staring you in the face. But it's not the same. It's all facade. All product placement. But the truth is you can't buy and sell free love. Can't brand it. Can't franchise it. All you can do is give it and accept it. Openly and honestly. Do you know what I mean, Dale? Do you know how to give love? (*taps the box*) Completely?

A beat as Dale tries to compute the last minute of his life. Enter Beth with a tray of coffees.

Beth: Here we go. Coffees all round.

Dale: Thank god.

Dale grabs a coffee, starts skolling it.

Beth: Jesus. Everything okay?

Dale: (*coughs*) Yep. All good.

Phillip: Yes, dandy, dear. Just dandy. In fact, I might leave you two to it. You don't want your old man hanging around.

Beth: Really?

Phillip: Yeah. Besides, your mother and I have some old friends coming round tonight. Better get home. Limber up.

Beth: Okay. Well, thanks, Dad. We really appreciate the help.

Phillip: Anything for my little girl. (*kisses Beth goodbye then nods to Dale*) Dale.

Dale: Phil … Phillips …

Phillip exits.

Beth: Wow. Phil, huh? You've made an impression.

Dale: An impression has been made.

Beth: So, what'd you say?

Dale: You know, I just explained. He was actually quite open-minded about it.

Beth: Really? So, there's nothing I need to worry about? No silly secrets? No list?

Long awkward beat.

Dale: Can't think of a thing.

Beth: Thank god. Could you imagine having to dodge that bullet every time he came around? Talk about awkward.

Dale: Yeah. Awkward.

A hug and kiss. Another nice moment.

Beth: So … where is my …

She taps the dildo box.

Dale: Buzz Lightyear?

Beth: You haven't lost him?

Dale: Bathroom. Third drawer.

Beth: Maybe we should take him out. Make sure he's still in one piece.

Dale: Now?

Beth: Why not? New place. A lot of rooms to break in.

Dale: Yes. A lot of rooms.

Beth: C'mon.

Beth exits. Dale lingers. He looks at the box, slightly disturbed.

Dale: Son of a bitch. The fridge!

ENDS

www.ingramcontent.com/pod-product-compliance
Lightning Source LLC
Chambersburg PA
CBHW070308010526
44107CB00056B/2528